PIANO · VOCAL · GUITAR

Great Hymns Treasury

ISBN 0-7935-7039-5

HAL•LEONARD®
CORPORATION

7777 W. BLUEMOUND RD. P.O. BOX 13819 MILWAUKEE, WI 53213

Visit Hal Leonard Online at
www.halleonard.com

Contents

A CHILD OF THE KING

Traditional

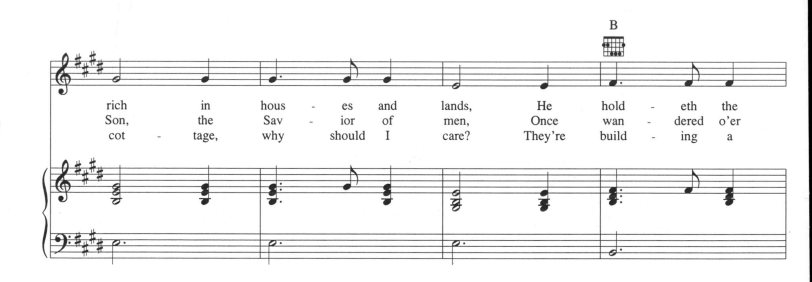

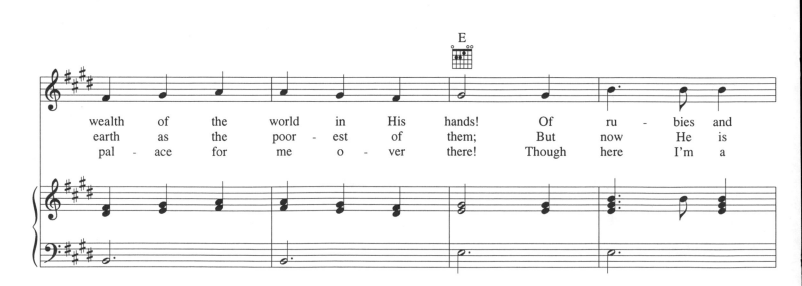

ABIDE WITH ME

Traditional

A - bide with me. Fast falls the e - ven - tide.
I need Thy pre - sence ev - 'ry pass - ing hour.

The dark - ness deep - ens, Lord, with me a - bide.
What but thy grace can foil the tempt - er's pow'r?

When oth - er help - ers fail and com - forts flee,
Who, like Thy - self, my guide and stay can be?

Help of the
Through cloud and

ALL CREATURES
OF OUR GOD AND KING

Traditional

ALL HAIL THE POWER OF JESUS' NAME

Traditional

All hail the power of Je - sus' name. Let an - gels pros - trate

fall. Bring forth the roy - al di - a - dem and

2. Let ev'ry kindred, ev'ry tribe on this terrestrial ball.
   To Him all majesty ascribe and crown Him Lord of all.
   To Him all majesty ascribe and crown Him Lord of all.

3. Oh, that with yonder sacred throng we at his feet may fall.
   We'll join the everlasting song and crown Him Lord of all.
   We'll join the everlasting song and crown Him Lord of all.

ALL THE WAY MY SAVIOR LEADS ME

Traditional

1. All the way my Sav - ior leads me; What have
2. way my Sav - ior leads me, Cheers each
3. way my Sav - ior leads me; O the

I to ask be - side? Can I doubt His ten - der
wind - ing path I tread, Gives me grace for ev - 'ry
ful - ness of His love! Per - fect rest to me is

mer - cy, Who through life has been my guide? Heav'n - ly
tri - al, Feeds me with the liv - ing bread. Though my
prom - ised In my Fa - ther's house a - bove. When my

AMAZING GRACE

Words by JOHN NEWTON
Traditional American Melody

Verse 3
And when this flesh and heart shall fail
and mortal life shall cease.
I shall possess within the veil
a life of joy and peace.

When we've been there ten thousand years,
bright shining as the sun.

We've no less days to sing God's praise
than when we first begun.

AT THE CROSS

Text by ISAAC WATTS
Music by RALPH E. HUDSON

BE THOU MY VISION

Traditional Irish

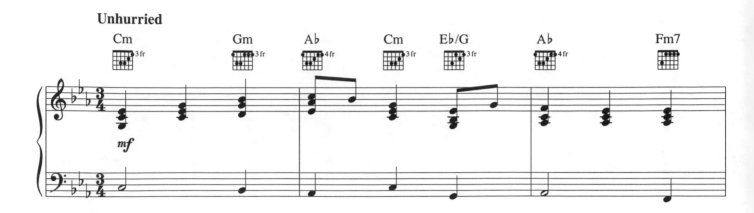

1. Be thou my _____ vi - sion, O
2. Be thou my _____ wis - dom, and
3. Great God of _____ heav - en, my

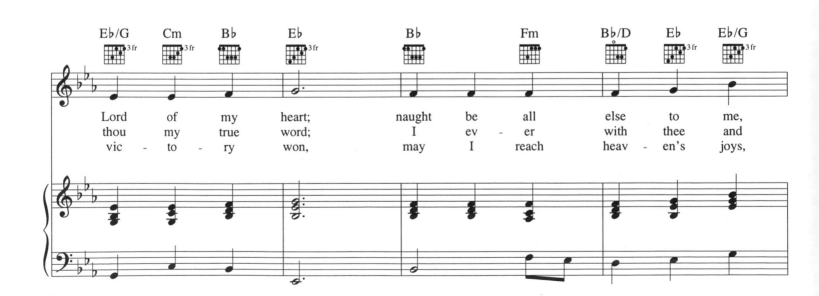

Lord of my heart; naught be all else to me,
thou my true word; I ev - er with thee and
vic - to - ry won, may I reach heav - en's joys,

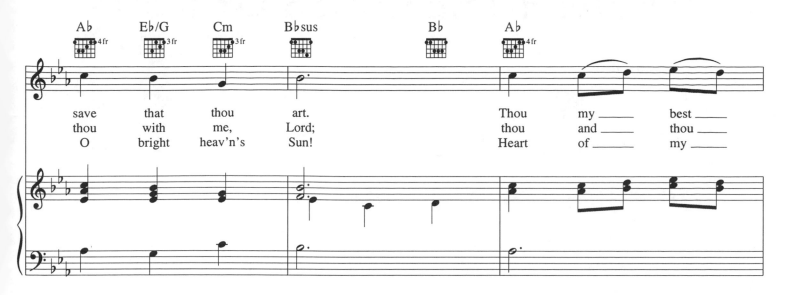

save that thou art.
thou with me, Lord;
O bright heav'n's Sun!

Thou my _____ best _____
thou and _____ thou _____
Heart of _____ my _____

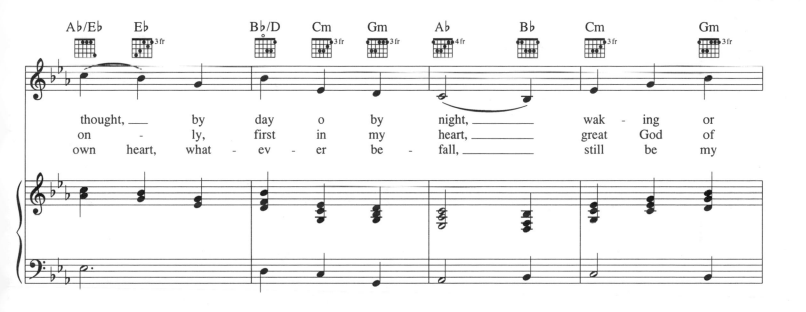

thought, _____ by day o by night, _____ wak - ing or
on - ly, first in my heart, _____ great God of
own heart, what - ev - er be - fall, _____ still be my

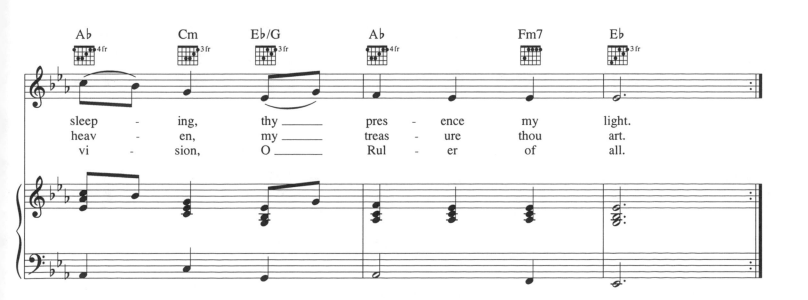

sleep - ing, thy _____ pres - ence my light.
heav - en, my _____ treas - ure thou art.
vi - sion, O _____ Rul - er of all.

BENEATH THE CROSS OF JESUS

Words by ELIZABETH C. CLEPHANE
Music by FREDERICK C. MAKER

BLEST BE THE TIE THAT BINDS

Traditional

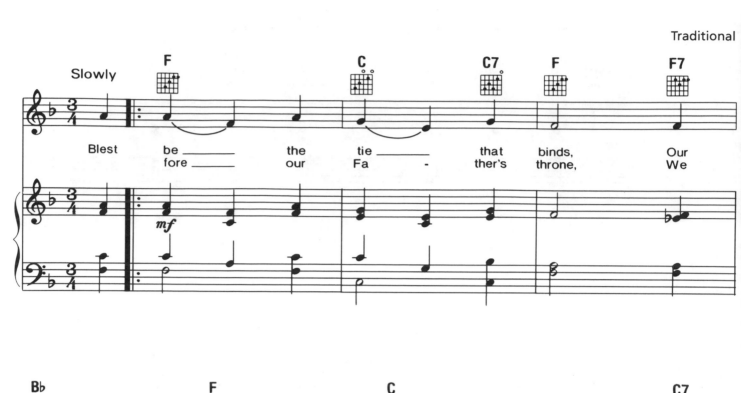

Blest be _____ the tie _____ that binds, Our
fore _____ our Fa - ther's throne, We

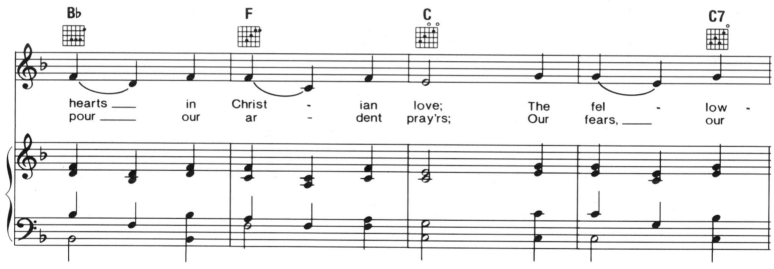

hearts _____ in Christ - ian love; The fel - low
pour _____ our ar - dent pray'rs; Our fears, _____ our

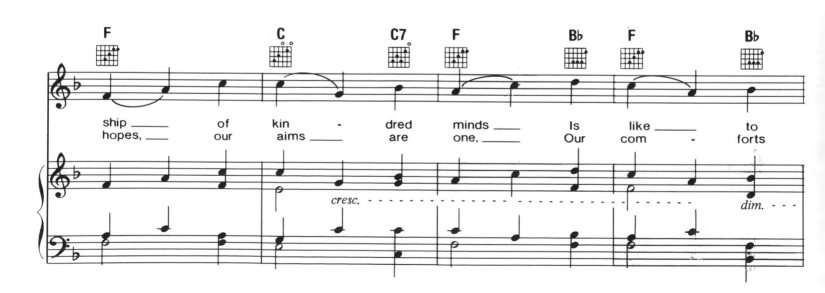

ship _____ of kin - dred minds _____ Is like _____ to
hopes, _____ our aims _____ are one, _____ Our com - forts

CLOSE TO THEE

Traditional

Moderately

1. Thou my ev - er - last - ing por - tion, more than friend or life to me, all a - long my pil - grim jour - ney, Sav - ior, let me walk with
2. ease or world - ly pleas - ure, nor for fame my prayer shall be; glad - ly will I toil and suf - fer, on - ly let me walk with
3. through the vale of shad - ows, bear me o'er life's fit - ful sea; then the gate of life e - ter - nal may I en - ter, Lord, with

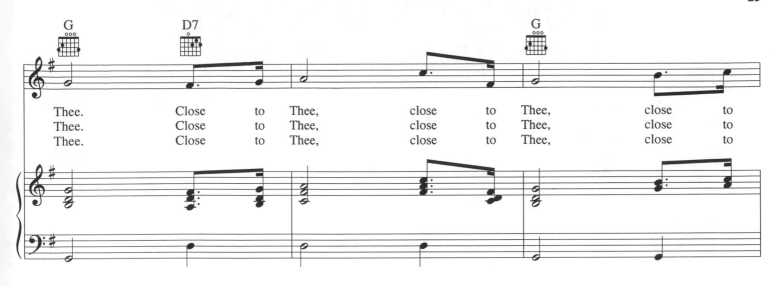

Thee. Close to Thee, close to Thee, close to
Thee. Close to Thee, close to Thee, close to
Thee. Close to Thee, close to Thee, close to

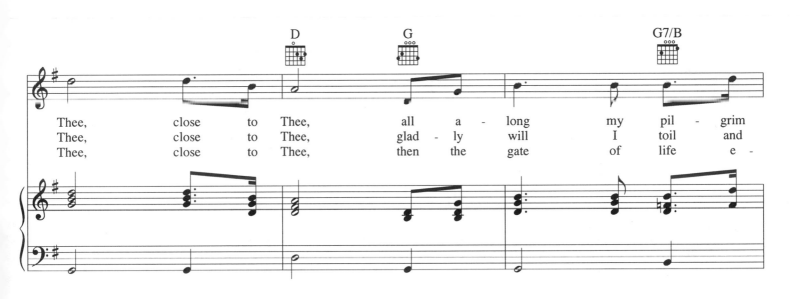

Thee, close to Thee, all a - long my pil - grim
Thee, close to Thee, glad - ly will I toil and
Thee, close to Thee, then the gate of life e -

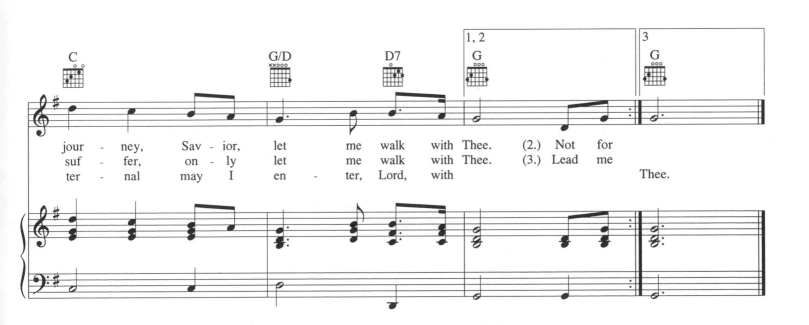

jour - ney, Sav - ior, let me walk with Thee. (2.) Not for
suf - fer, on - ly let me walk with Thee. (3.) Lead me
ter - nal may I en - ter, Lord, with Thee.

COME, THOU FOUNT OF EVERY BLESSING

Words by ROBERT ROBINSON
Traditional Music compiled by WYETH

FOOTSTEPS TO JESUS

Traditional

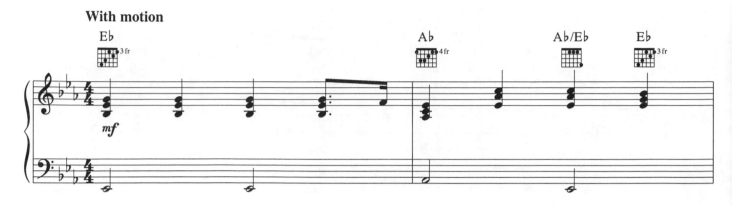

With motion

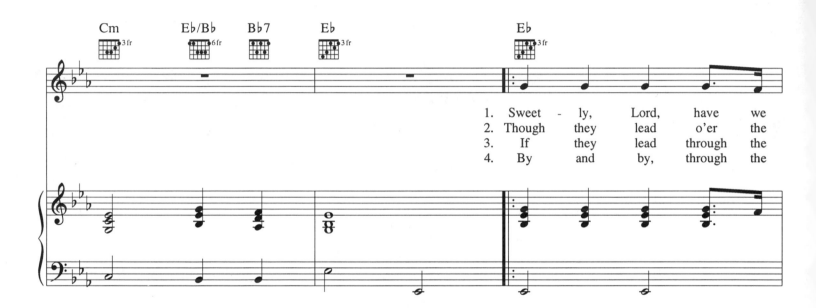

1. Sweet - ly, Lord, have we
2. Though they lead o'er the
3. If they lead through the
4. By and by, through the

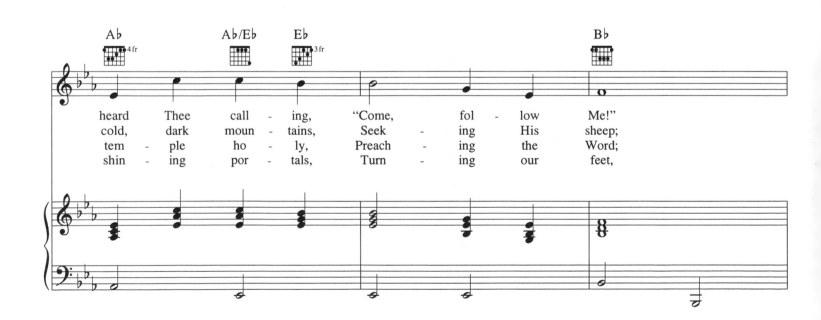

heard Thee call - ing, "Come, fol - low Me!"
cold, dark moun - tains, Seek - ing His sheep;
tem - ple ho - ly, Preach - ing the Word;
shin - ing por - tals, Turn - ing our feet,

FOR THE BEAUTY OF THE EARTH

Text by FOLLIOT S. PIERPOINT
Music by CONRAD KOCHER

*for Holy Communion

GOD OF GRACE
AND GOD OF GLORY

Text by HARRY EMERSON FOSDICK
Music by JOHN HUGHES

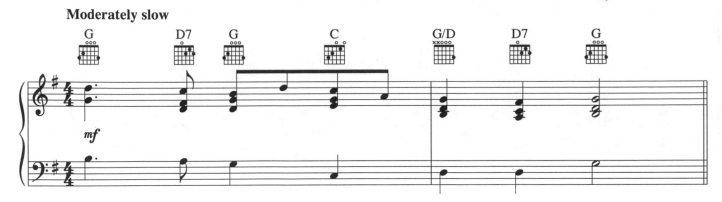

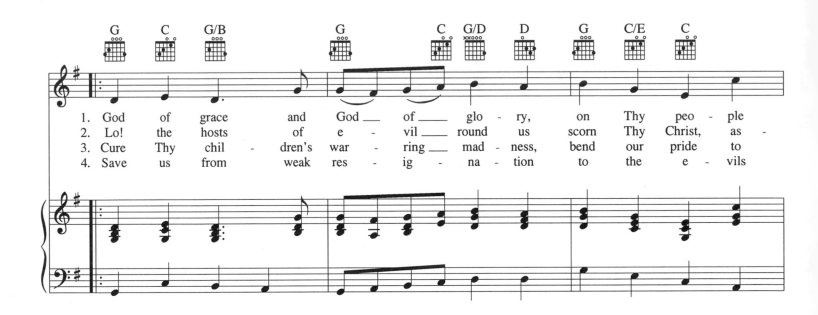

1. God of grace and God of glory, on Thy peo - ple
2. Lo! the hosts of e - vil round us scorn Thy Christ, as -
3. Cure Thy chil - dren's war - ring mad - ness, bend our pride to
4. Save us from weak res - ig - na - tion to the e - vils

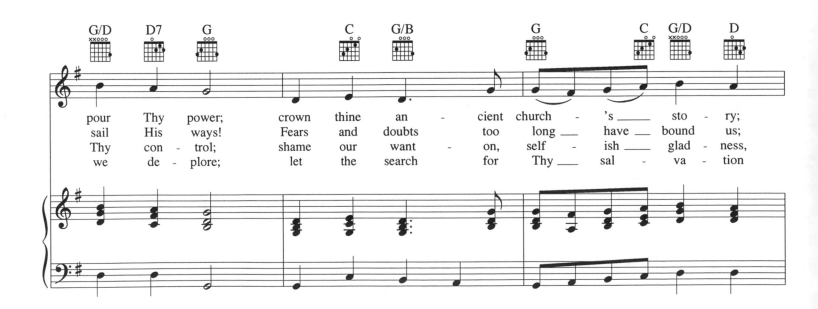

pour Thy power; crown thine an - cient church - 's sto - ry;
sail His ways! Fears and doubts too long have bound us;
Thy con - trol; shame our want - on, self - ish glad - ness,
we de - plore; let the search for Thy sal - va - tion

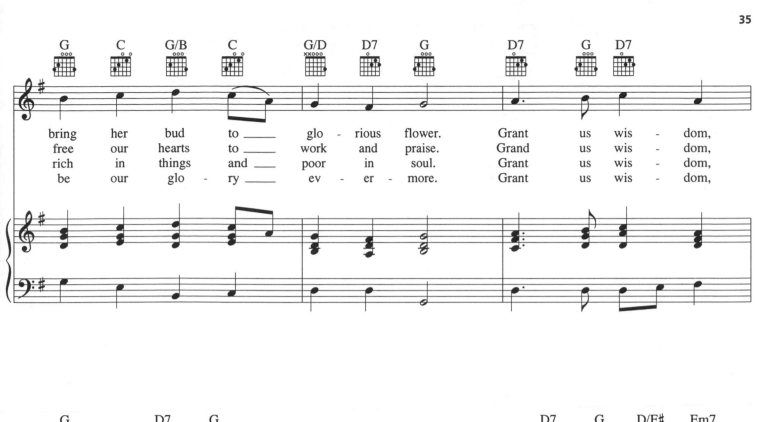

bring her bud to _____ glo - rious flower. Grant us wis - dom,
free our hearts to _____ work and praise. Grand us wis - dom,
rich in things and _____ poor in soul. Grant us wis - dom,
be our glo - ry _____ ev - er - more. Grant us wis - dom,

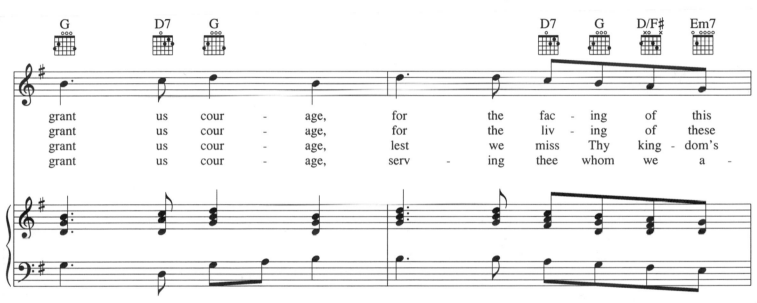

grant us cour - age, for the fac - ing of this
grant us cour - age, for the liv - ing of these
grant us cour - age, lest we miss Thy king - dom's
grant us cour - age, serv - ing thee whom we a -

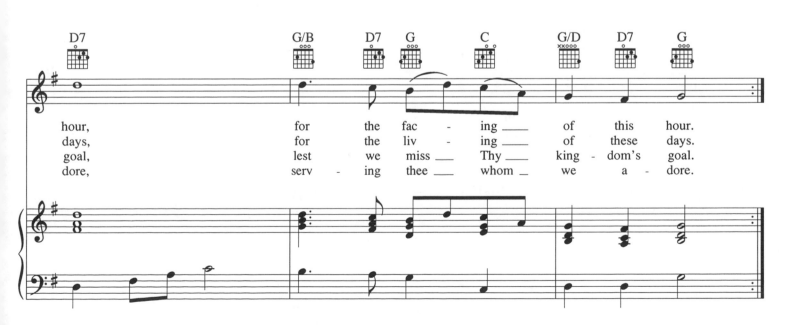

hour, for the fac - ing _____ of this hour.
days, for the liv - ing _____ of these days.
goal, lest we miss ____ Thy ____ king - dom's goal.
dore, serv - ing thee ____ whom __ we a - dore.

GOD OF OUR FATHERS

Words and Music by DANIEL C. ROBERTS
and GEORGE WARREN

8va

HAVE THINE OWN WAY LORD

Words by ADELAIDE POLLARD
Music by GEORGE STEBBINS

HE HIDETH MY SOUL

Words by FANNY J. CROSBY
Music by WILLIAM J. KIRKPATRICK

HIS EYE IS ON THE SPARROW

By MRS. S.A. MARTIN

HOLY, HOLY, HOLY!
LORD GOD ALMIGHTY

Text by REGINALD HEBER
Music by JOHN B. DYKES

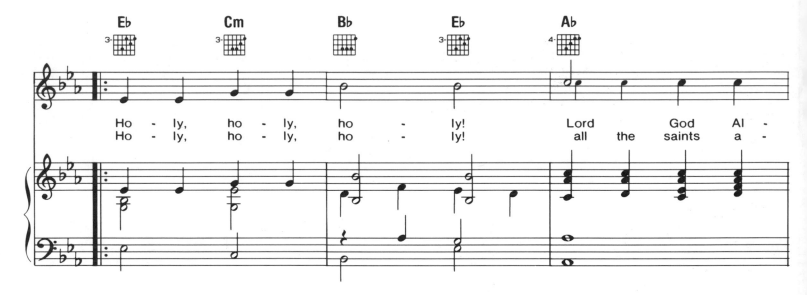

Ho - ly, ho - ly, ho - ly! Lord God Al -
Ho - ly, ho - ly, ho - ly! all the saints a -

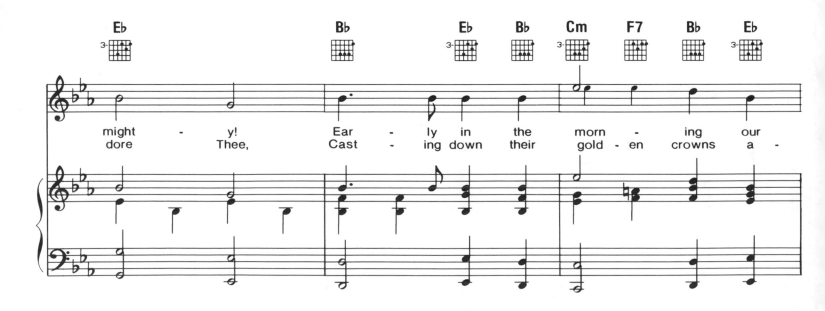

might - y! Ear - ly in the morn - ing our
dore Thee, Cast - ing down their gold - en crowns a -

PRAISE TO THE LORD, THE ALMIGHTY

Traditional

HOW FIRM A FOUNDATION

Traditional text compiled by JOHN RIPPON
Traditional music compiled by JOSEPH FUNK

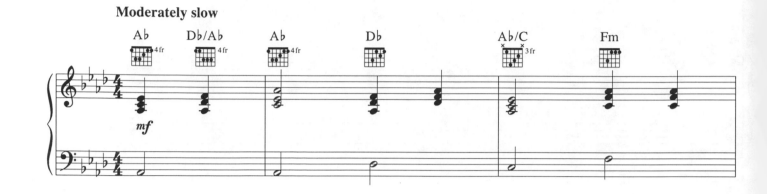

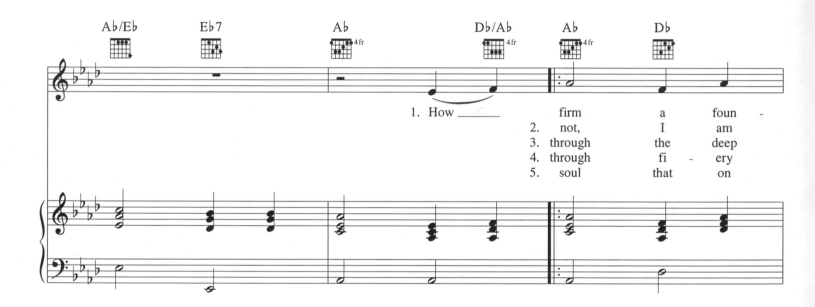

1. How _____ firm a foun-
2. not, I am
3. through the deep
4. through fi - ery
5. soul that on

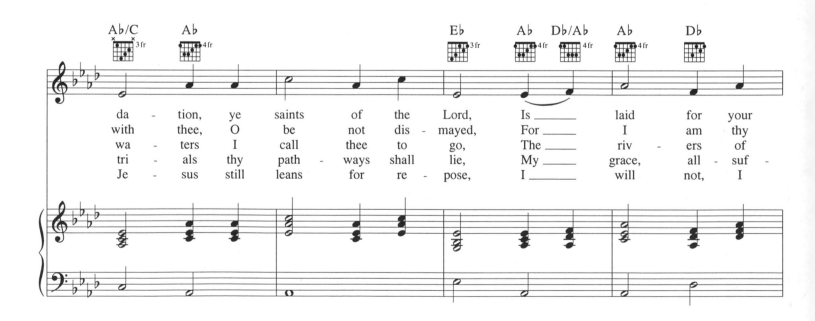

da - tion, ye saints of the Lord, Is _____ laid for your
with thee, O be not dis - mayed, For _____ I am thy
wa - ters I call thee to go, The _____ riv - ers of
tri - als thy path - ways shall lie, My _____ grace, all - suf-
Je - sus still leans for re - pose, I _____ will not, I

HOW SWEET THE NAME OF JESUS SOUNDS

Words by JOHN NEWTON
Music by ALEXANDER RAINAGLE

I LOVE THY KINGDOM, LORD

Words by TIM DWIGHT
Music by AARON WILLIAMS

I LOVE TO TELL THE STORY

By K. HANKEY
and W.G. FISCHER

IMMORTAL, INVISIBLE

Traditional

With strength

1. Im - mor - tal, in -
2. rest - ing, un -
3. all, life Thou
4. reign - est in

vis - i - ble, God on - ly wise, In
hast - ing, and si - lent as light, In Nor
giv - est, to both great and small; In
glo - ry; Thou dwell - est in light; Thine

light in - ac - ces - si - ble hid from our
want - ing nor wast - ing, Thou rul - est in
all life Thou liv - est, the true life of
an - gels a - dore Thee, all veil - ing their

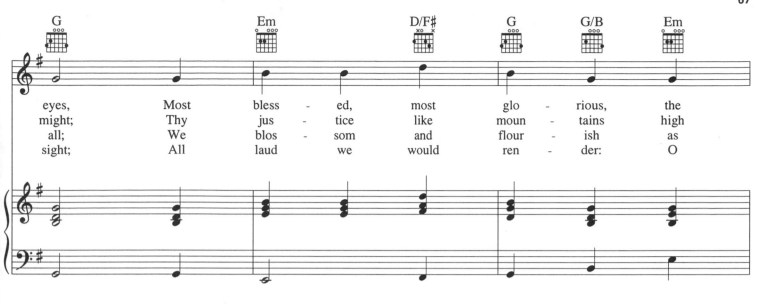

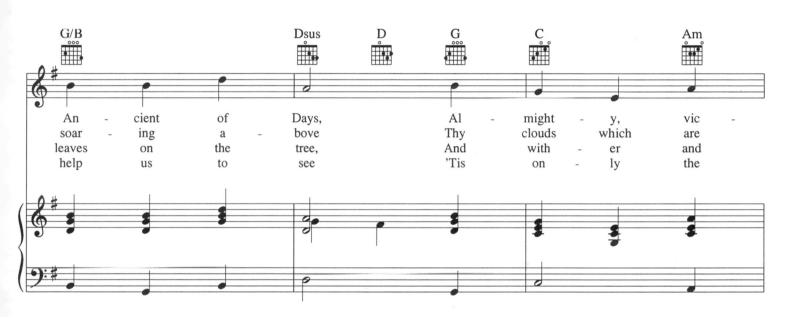

IN THE GARDEN

Words and Music by
C. AUSTIN MILES

Flowing

I come to the gar-den a - lone, _____ while the
speaks, and the sound of His voice _____ is so

dew is still on the ros - es; and the voice I
sweet the birds hush their sing - ing; and the mel - o -

hear, fall-ing on my ear, the Son of God dis -
- dy that He gave to me with - in my heart is

IT IS WELL WITH MY SOUL

Text by HORATIO G. SPAFFORD
Music by PHILIP P. BLISS

JESUS, LOVER OF MY SOUL

Traditional

JESUS PAID IT ALL

Traditional

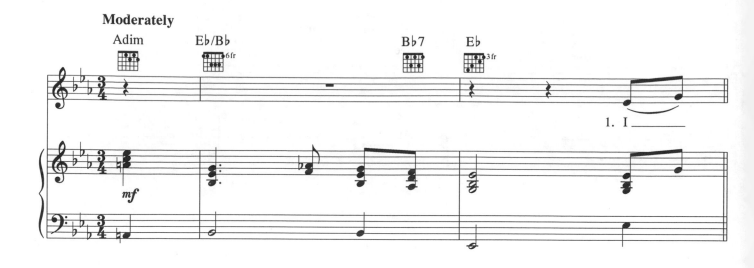

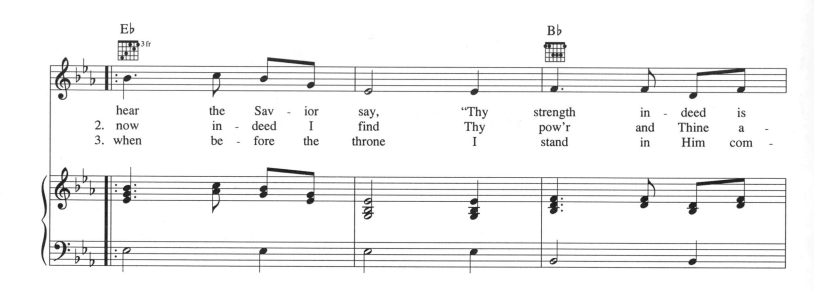

JUST A CLOSER WALK WITH THEE

Traditional
Arranged by KENNETH MORRIS

3. When my feeble life is o'er,
   Time for me will be no more;
   On that bright eternal shore
   I will walk, dear Lord, close to Thee.

THE LILY OF THE VALLEY

Traditional

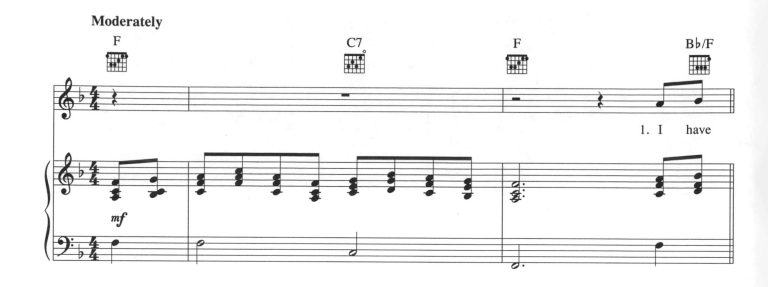

found a friend in Je - sus, He's ev - 'ry - thing to me, He's the
2. all my grief has tak - en, and all my sor - rows borne; In temp -
3. nev - er, nev - er leave me, nor yet for - sake me here, While I

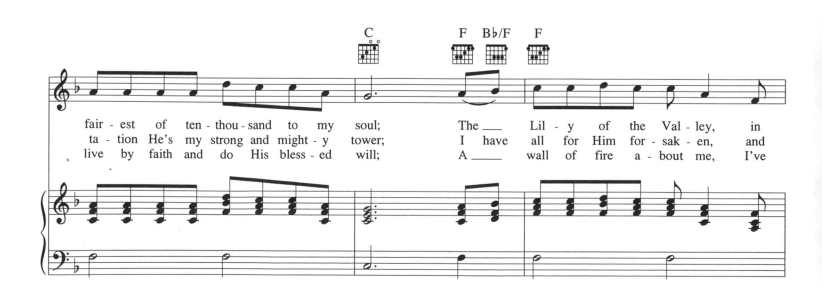

fair - est of ten - thou - sand to my soul; The ___ Lil - y of the Val - ley, in
ta - tion He's my strong and might - y tower; I have all for Him for - sak - en, and
live by faith and do His bless - ed will; A ___ wall of fire a - bout me, I've

LOVE LIFTED ME

By JAMES ROWE
and HOWARD E. SMITH

MY FAITH HAS FOUND A RESTING PLACE

Traditional

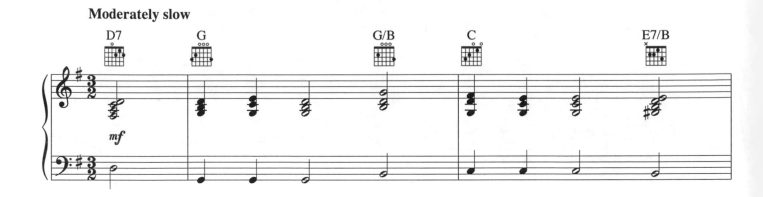

Moderately slow

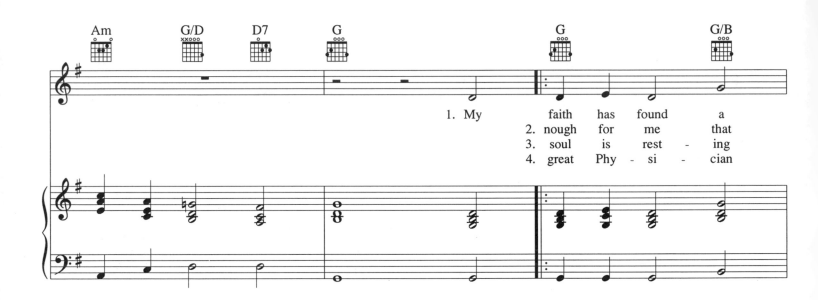

1. My faith has found a
2. nough for me that
3. soul is rest - ing
4. great Phy - si - cian

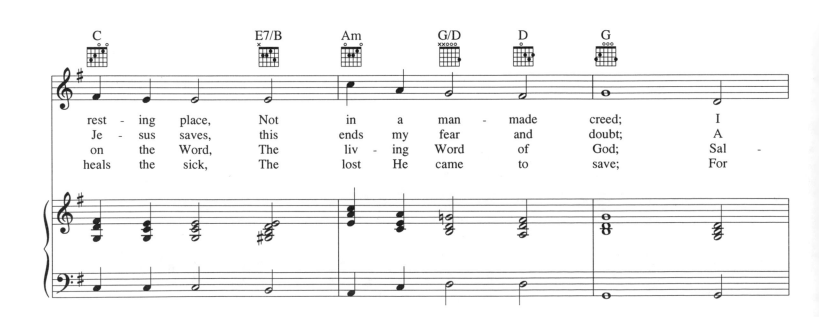

rest - ing place, Not in a man - made creed; I
Je - sus saves, this ends my fear and doubt; A
on the Word, The liv - ing Word of God; Sal -
heals the sick, The lost He came to save; For

MY FAITH LOOKS UP TO THEE

Traditional

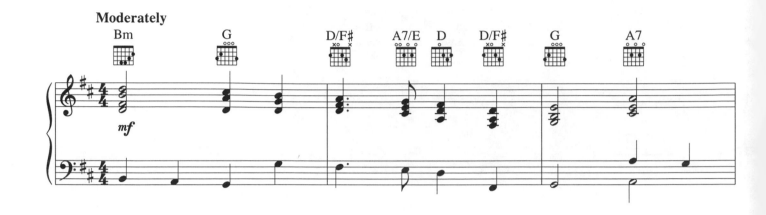

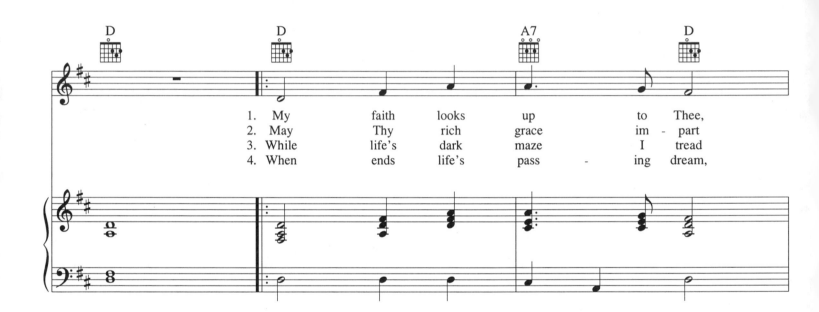

1. My faith looks up to Thee,
2. May Thy rich grace im - part
3. While life's dark maze I tread
4. When ends life's pass - ing dream,

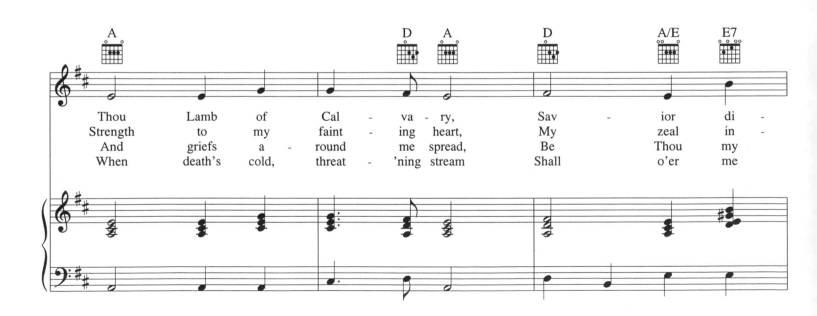

Thou Lamb of Cal - va - ry, Sav - ior di -
Strength to my faint - ing heart, My zeal in -
And griefs a - round me spread, Be Thou my
When death's cold, threat - 'ning stream Shall o'er me

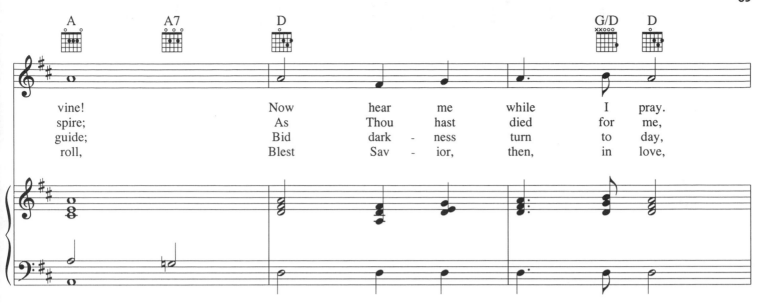

vine!   Now   hear   me   while   I   pray.
spire;   As   Thou   hast   died   for   me,
guide;   Bid   dark - ness   turn   to   day,
roll,   Blest   Sav - ior,   then,   in   love,

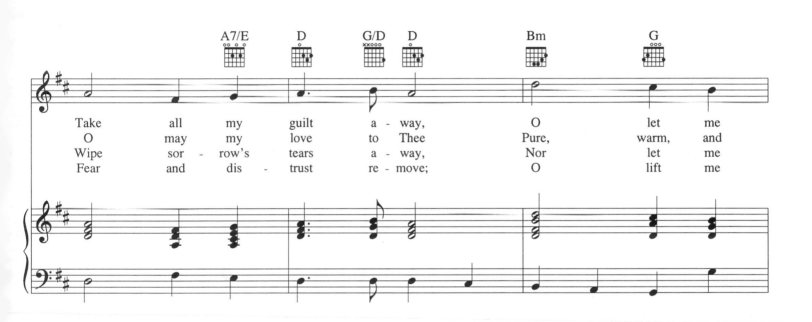

Take   all   my   guilt   a - way,   O   let   me
O   may   my   love   to   Thee   Pure,   warm,   and
Wipe   sor - row's   tears   a - way,   Nor   let   me
Fear   and   dis - trust   re - move;   O   lift   me

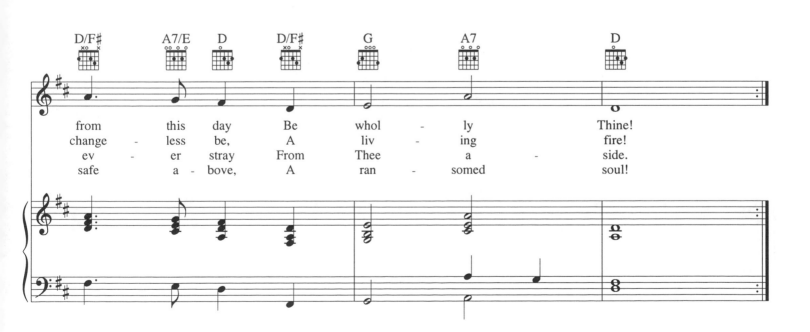

from   this   day,   Be   whol - ly   Thine!
change - less   be,   A   liv - ing   fire!
ev - er   stray   From   Thee   a - side.
safe   a - bove,   A   ran - somed   soul!

NEAR THE CROSS

Traditional

moun - tain.
round me.
o'er me.
riv - er.

In the cross, in the cross

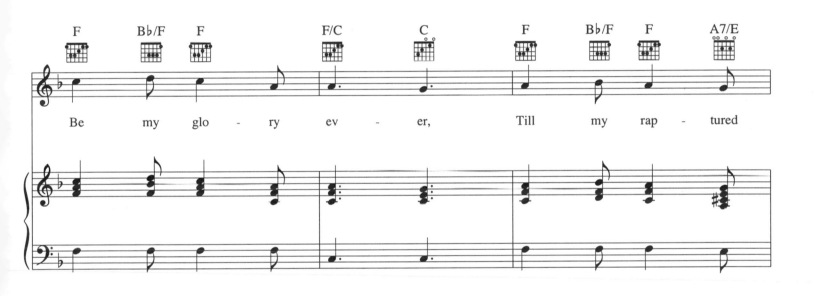

Be my glo - ry ev - er, Till my rap - tured

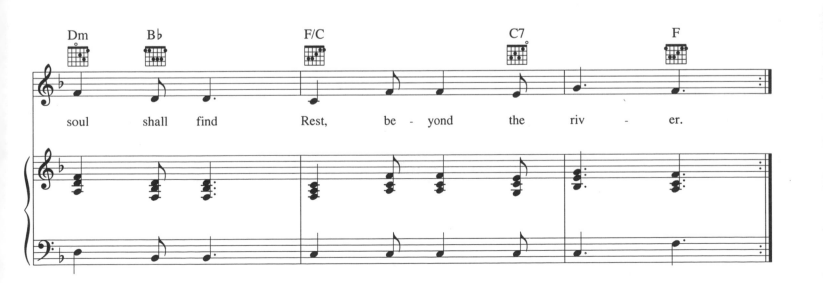

soul shall find Rest, be - yond the riv - er.

NEAR TO THE HEART OF GOD

Traditional

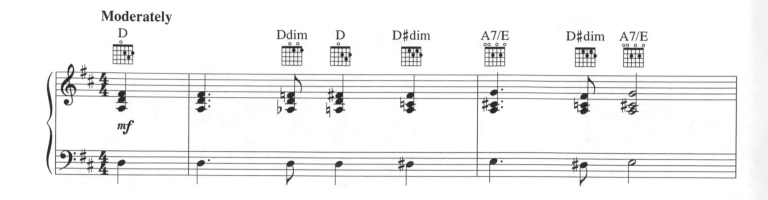

1. There is a place of
2. is a place of
3. is a place of

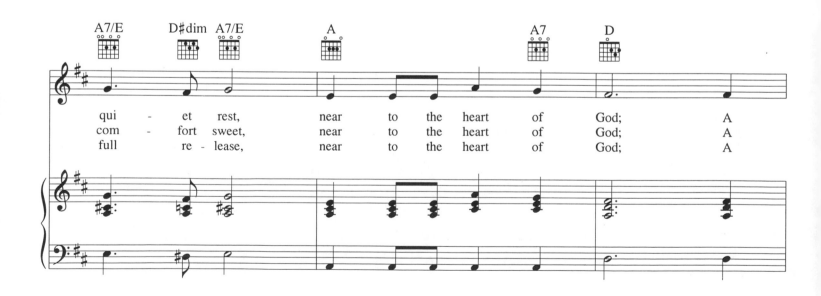

quiet rest, near to the heart of God; A
comfort sweet, near to the heart of God; A A
full release, near to the heart of God; A A

O FOR A THOUSAND TONGUES TO SING

Text by CHARLES WESLEY
Music by CARL G. GLASER

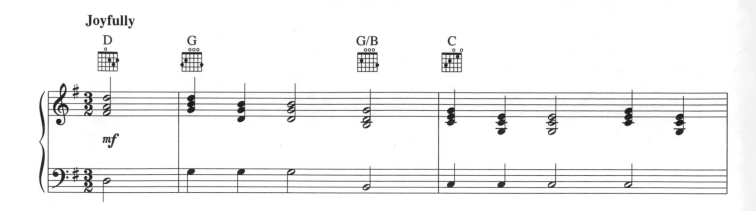

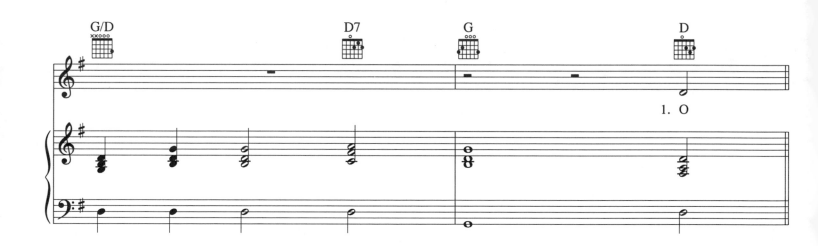

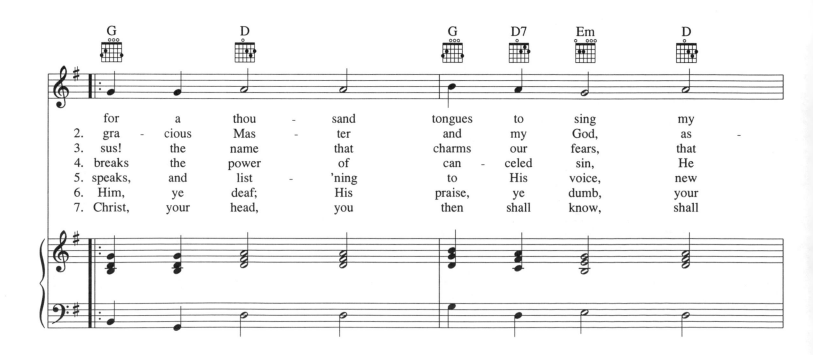

1. O for a thou - sand tongues to sing my
2. gra - cious Mas - ter and my God, as -
3. sus! the name that charms our fears, that
4. breaks the power of can - celed sin, He
5. speaks, and list - 'ning to His voice, new
6. Him, ye deaf; His praise, ye dumb, your
7. Christ, your head, you then shall know, shall

O GOD OUR HELP IN AGES PAST

Traditional

93

O MASTER,
LET ME WALK WITH THEE

Traditional

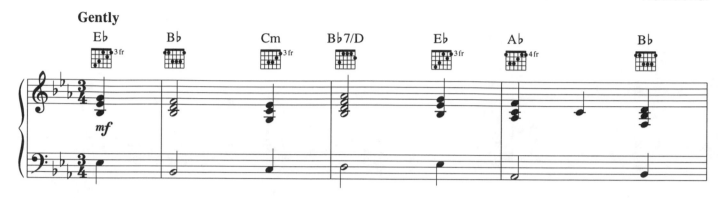

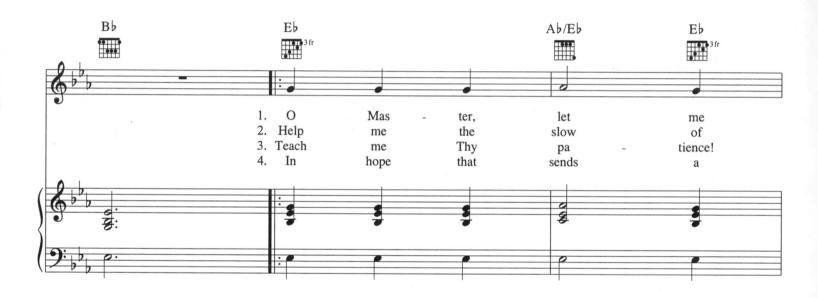

1. O   Mas - ter,   let   me
2. Help   me   the   slow   of
3. Teach   me   Thy   pa -   tience!
4. In   hope   that   sends   a

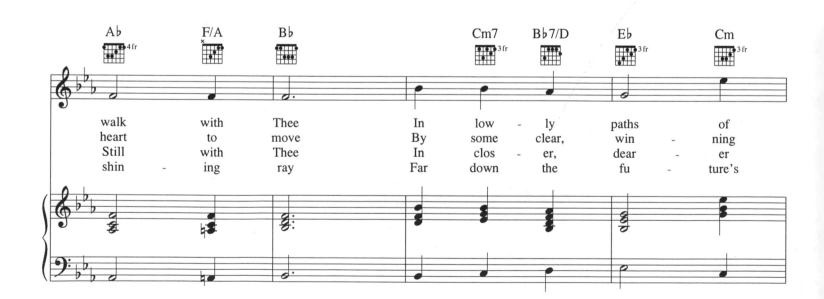

walk   with   Thee   In   low - ly   paths   of
heart   to   move   By   some   clear,   win - ning
Still   with   Thee   In   clos - er,   dear - er
shin - ing   ray   Far   down   the   fu - ture's

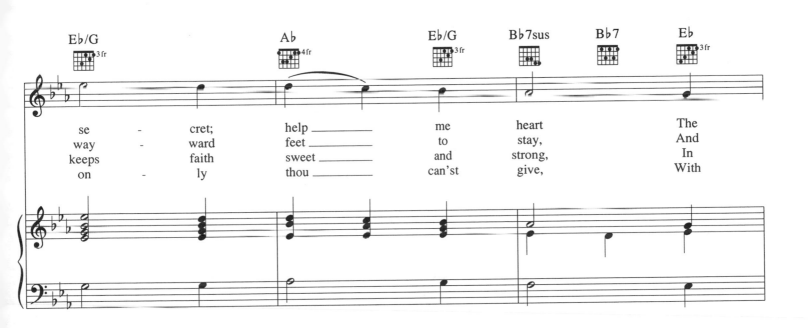

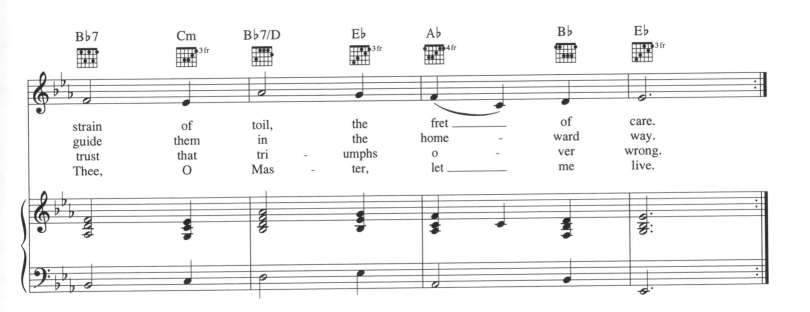

THE OLD RUGGED CROSS

Traditional

PRECIOUS MEMORIES

Traditional Spiritual

3. As I travel on life's pathway, I know not what life shall hold;
   As I wander hopes grow fonder, Precious mem'ries flood my soul.

SAVIOR LIKE A SHEPHERD LEAD US

Traditional

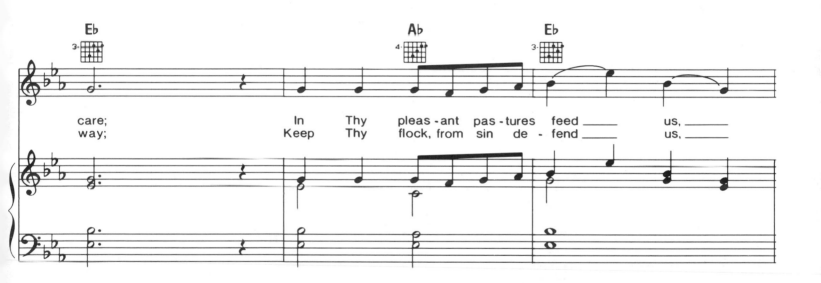

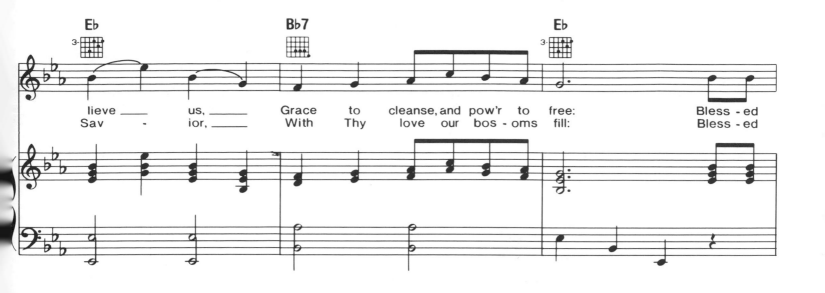

lieve ____ us, ____ Grace to cleanse, and pow'r to free: Bless - ed
Sav - ior, ____ With Thy love our bos - oms fill: Bless - ed

Je - sus, Bless - ed Je - sus, Ear - ly let us turn to Thee; Bless - ed
Je - sus, Bless - ed Je - sus, Thou hast loved us, love us still; Bless - ed

Fine   D.S. al Fine

Je - sus, Bless - ed Je - sus, Ear - ly let us turn to Thee.
Je - sus, Bless - ed Je - sus, Thou hast loved us, love us still.

REJOICE, THE LORD IS KING

Traditional

RING THE BELLS OF HEAVEN

Traditional

1. Ring the bells of heav - en! There is joy to - day,
2. Ring the bells of heav - en! There is joy to - day,
3. Ring the bells of heav - en! Spread the feast to - day!

For a soul, re - turn - ing from the wild!
For the wan - derer now is rec - on - ciled;
An - gels swell the glad tri - um - phant strain!

See, the Fa - ther meets him out up - on the way,
Yes, a soul is res - cued from his sin - ful way,
Tell the joy - ful tid - ings, Bear it far a - way!

SOFTLY AND TENDERLY

By WILL L. THOMPSON

Moderately Slow

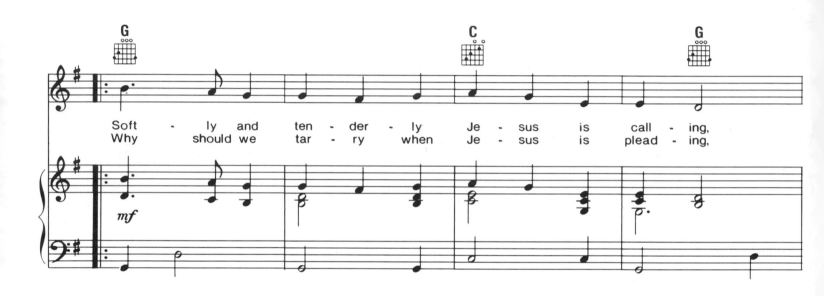

Soft - ly and ten - der - ly Je - sus is call - ing,
Why should we tar - ry when Je - sus is plead - ing,

mf

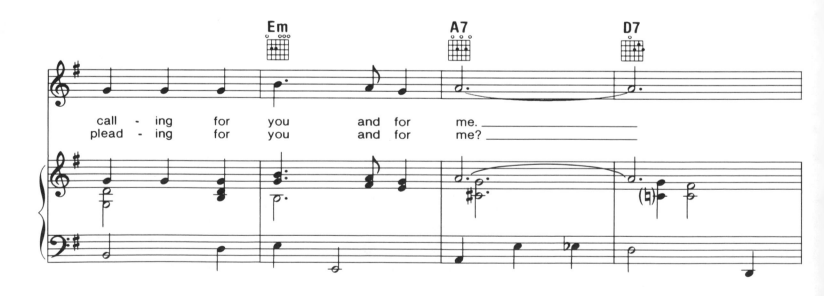

call - ing for you and for me. _____
plead - ing for you and for me? _____

SPIRIT OF GOD
DESCEND UPON MY HEART

Traditional

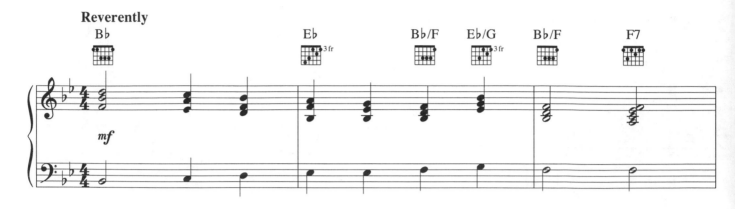

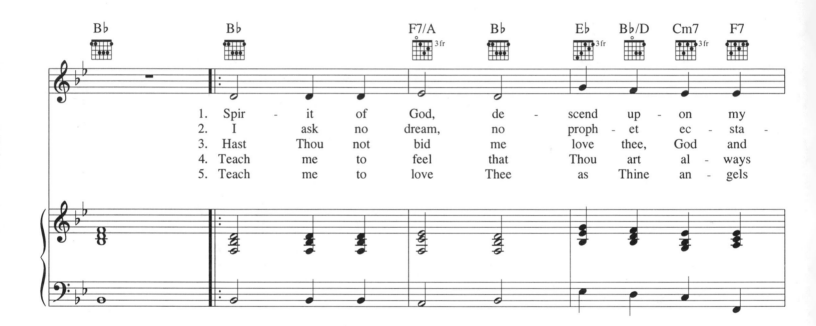

1. Spir - it of God, de - scend up - on my
2. I ask no dream, no proph - et ec - sta -
3. Hast Thou not bid me love thee, God and
4. Teach me to feel that Thou art al - ways
5. Teach me to love Thee as Thine an - gels

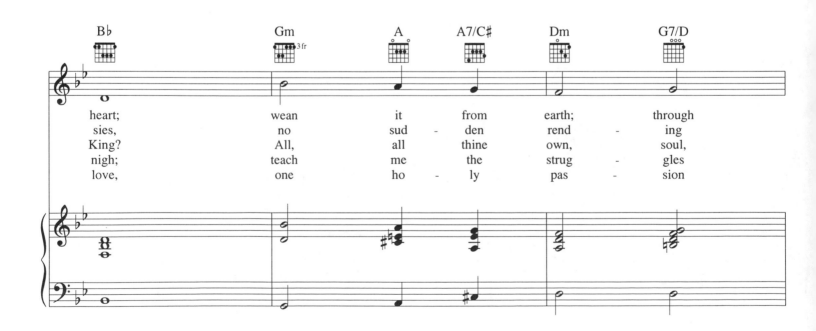

heart;   wean   it   from   earth;   through
sies,   no   sud - den   rend - ing
King?   All,   all   thine   own,   soul,
nigh;   teach   me   the   strug - gles
love,   one   ho - ly   pas - sion

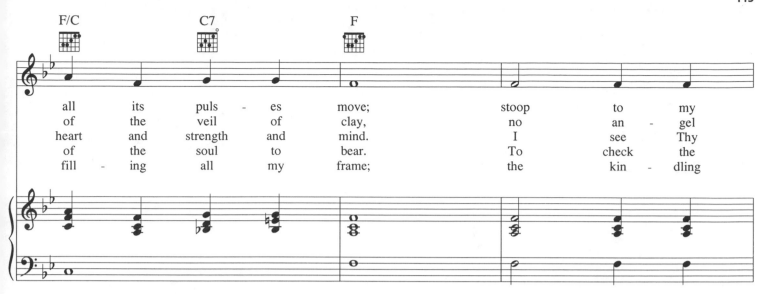

all its puls - es move; stoop to my
of the veil of clay, no an - gel
heart and strength and mind. I see Thy
of the soul to bear. To check the
fill - ing all my frame; the kin - dling

weak - ness, might - y as Thou art,
vis - i - tant, no o - pening skies;
cross; there teach my heart to cling.
ris - ing doubt, the reb - el sigh,
of the heaven - de - scend - ed Dove,

and make me love Thee as I ought to love.
but take the dim - ness of my soul a - way.
O let me seek Thee, and O let me find!
teach me the pa - tience of un - an - swered prayer.
my heart an al - tar, and Thy love the flame.

THERE IS A BALM IN GILEAD

Traditional

THIS IS MY FATHER'S WORLD

Words by MALTBIE BABCOCK
Traditional Music

WE'RE MARCHING TO ZION/
WHEN THE SAINTS GO MARCHING IN

We're Marching to Zion

Traditional

beau-ti-ful, beau-ti-ful Zi - on. We're march-ing up-ward to Zi - on, ___ the

beau-ti-ful cit-y of God. We're God.

When the Saints Go Marching In

Words by Katherine E. Purvis
Music by James M. Black

Oh when the saints ___

'TIS SO SWEET TO TRUST IN JESUS

Traditional

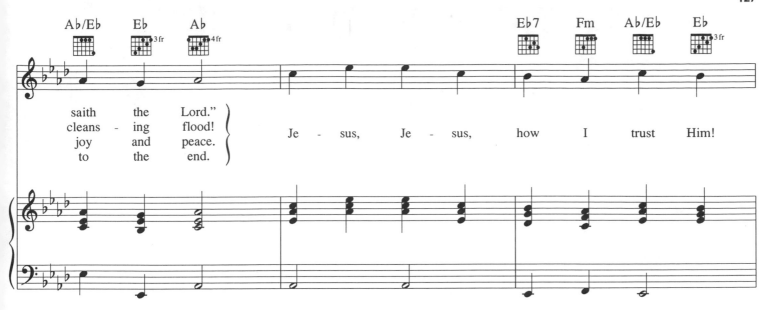

saith the Lord."
cleans - ing flood!
joy to the end.

Je - sus, Je - sus, how I trust Him!

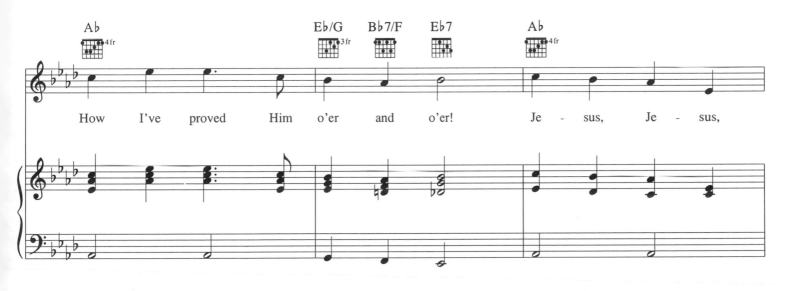

How I've proved Him o'er and o'er! Je - sus, Je - sus,

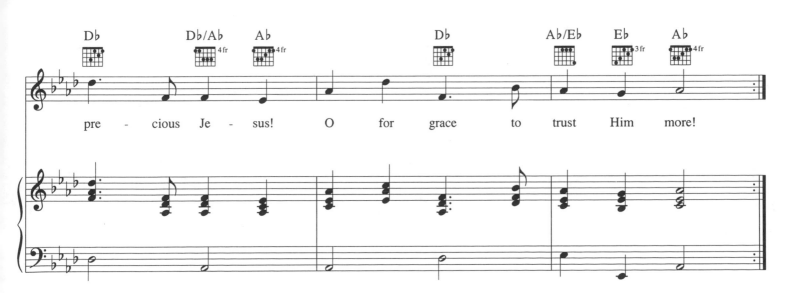

pre - cious Je - sus! O for grace to trust Him more!

TO GOD BE THE GLORY

Traditional

WONDERFUL WORDS OF LIFE

Traditional

1. Sing them o - ver a - gain to me,
2. Christ, the bless - ed One, gives to all
3. Sweet - ly ech - o the gos - pel call,

Won - der - ful words of Life; _____ Let me more of their
Won - der - ful words of Life; _____ Sin - ner, listen to the
Won - der - ful words of Life; _____ Of - fer par - don and

beau - ty see, Won - der - ful words of Life.
lov - ing call, Won - der - full words of Life.
peace to all, Won - der - ful words of Life.

WONDROUS LOVE

Traditional

1. What won-drous love is this, O my soul, O my
2. won-drous love is this, O my soul, O I my
3. God and to the Lamb, I will sing, I will
4. when from death I'm free, I'll sing on, I'll sing

soul! What won-drous love is this, O my soul! What
soul! What won-drous love is this, O my soul! What
sing, to God and to the Lamb, I will sing. To
on, and when from death I'm free, I'll sing on. And

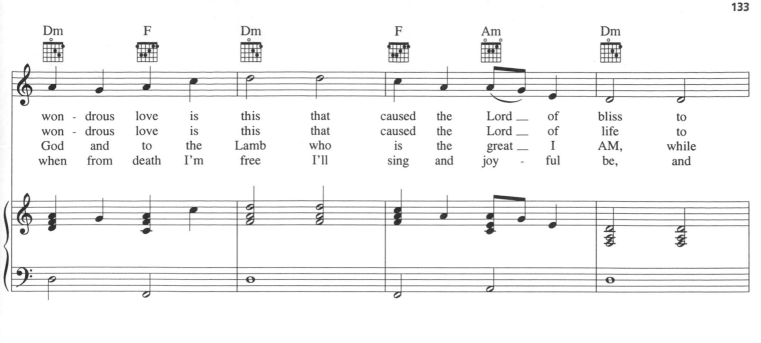

won - drous love is this that caused the Lord __ of bliss to
won - drous love is this that caused the Lord __ of life to
God and to the Lamb who is the great __ I AM, while
when from death I'm free I'll sing and joy - ful be, and

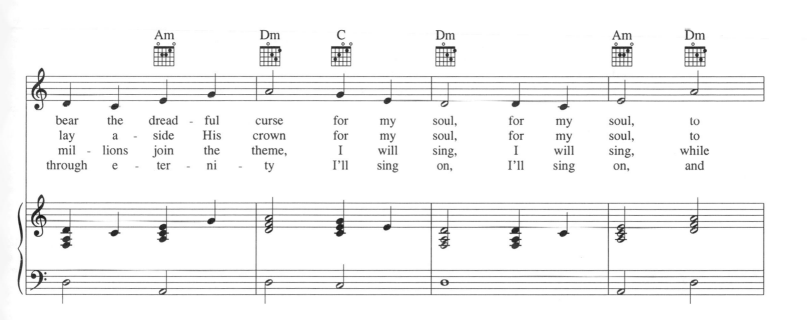

bear the dread - ful curse for my soul, for my soul, to
lay a - side His crown for my soul, for my soul, to
mil - lions join the theme, I will sing, I will sing, while
through e - ter - ni - ty I'll sing on, I'll sing on, and

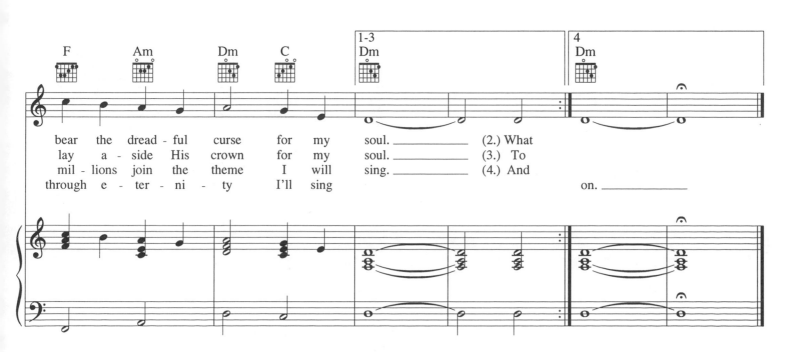

bear the dread - ful curse for my soul. ____ (2.) What
lay a - side His crown for my soul. ____ (3.) To
mil - lions join the theme I will sing. ____ (4.) And
through e - ter - ni - ty I'll sing on. ____

WERE YOU THERE?

Traditional Spiritual

Moderately

Were you   there   when they cru - ci - fied   my Lord? (Were   you   there?)   Were   you
there   when they nailed Him to   the   tree? (To   the   tree?)   Were   you
there   when they pierced Him in   the   side? (In   the   side?)   Were   you

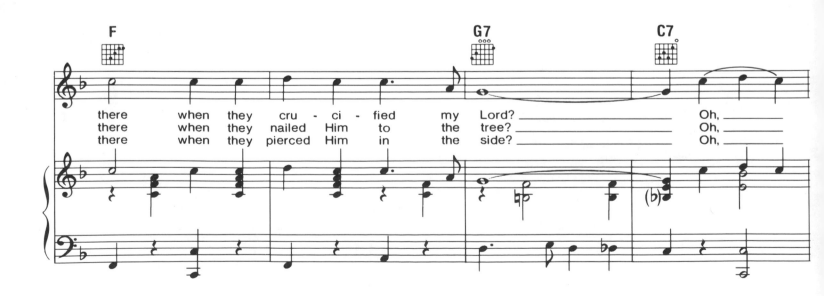

there   when they cru - ci - fied   my   Lord? _____ Oh, _____
there   when they nailed Him to   the   tree? _____ Oh, _____
there   when they pierced Him in   the   side? _____ Oh, _____